WELCOME SPEECHES
and More

Carole Cupples

D1275069

Abingdon Press

WELCOME SPEECHES AND MORE

Copyright © 1993 by Abingdon Press

This book is printed on acid-free, recycled paper.

ISBN 0-687-27192-4

Scripture quotations, except for brief paraphrases, or unless otherwise noted, are from the New Revised Standard Version Bible, Copyright 1989 by the Division of Christian Education of the National Council of the Churches of Christ in the USA, or from the Revised Standard Version of the Bible, copyright 1946, 1952, 1971 by the Division of Christian Education of the National Council of Churches of Christ in the USA. Used by permission.

Special thanks to Mrs. Betty Butler for the ideas for the Choir Day Address on p. 37.

97 98 99 00 01 02 — 10 9 8 7 6

MANUFACTURED IN THE UNITED STATES OF AMERICA

CONTENTS

INTRODUCTION

There are many times when a special need occurs in the life of our churches. You may have been called on to welcome guests to a program, honor your pastor on his or her anniversary, or pay tribute to someone who has died. There are ideas here for these, as well as other special occasions.

I have been operating a Christian bookstore for sixteen years. During those years many times customers have come in needing help with programs in their churches. As a result of my attempt and desire to meet those needs, I offer to you this book. My humble prayer is that it will assist you in your ministry.

Encouragement has come to me from friends, coworkers, and especially my husband, Rick. However, the seed of inspiration was planted by a dear Christian woman, Mrs. Pearl Anthony, who now lives in heaven with her Lord. She could have taken the ideas I have given here and presented programs to honor and glorify God. May these ideas help you to do likewise.

GENERAL WELCOME SPEECHES

Welcome to Worship

Pastor, visiting pastors, distinguished guests, fellow worshipers *(and _____)*,

I wish to welcome you here today to participate fully in our program. As the scripture says, "The Spirit and the bride say, 'Come.' And let everyone who hears say, 'Come.' And let everyone who is thirsty come. Let anyone who wishes take the water of life as a gift" (Rev. 22:17). So *come* with us today to worship our precious Lord and Savior. He is worthy of our worship! You are welcome here today not really because of anything we can do or have done, although every provision is made for your comfort, but because of that worthy Savior who has made a way and welcomed us into his Family. That is why you are welcome, welcome once, welcome twice, and welcome once again!

Welcome to a Celebration

Pastors, leaders, friends, Christian brothers and sisters, ladies and gentlemen *(and _____)*,

We welcome you here today to celebrate this auspicious occasion.

The word "welcome" contains a rich meaning, and to welcome you here today for our program, we want to illustrate some of that meaning:

(Small children may carry the letters while you speak. Older children may wish to say the word and the speech with each letter.)

W—Warm: May you find among us warm smiles.

E—Each: Each of us desires to make you welcome.

L—Love: It is the love of God shed abroad in our hearts that we want you to feel.

C—Comfort: It is our desire that everything possible be provided for your comfort.

O—Others: The Bible says in Philippians 2:3, "Regard others as better than yourselves." It is our desire to put Jesus first, others second, that's you, and ourselves last.

M—Many: May you receive many blessings here today.

E—Ever: May you ever remember the welcome you received from us today.

W E L C O M E !

Welcome to Worship

Come naked, come filthy, come ragged, come poor, come wretched, come just as you are.

Pastor, visiting pastors, distinguished guests, fellow worshipers *(and _____)*,

Welcome! Welcome to one and all. As we sit here today we are dressed in fine clothes, blessed with shelter from the heat *(or cold)* in this beautiful building, and well fed from the abundance of our land. Because of just these things it is easy to welcome you and to offer to you every comfort and convenience at our disposal.

But the question occurs to me, Are we welcome in God's eyes? Beyond the fine clothes, proper behavior, health, and well-being we see, what does God see in us today?

I believe that he sees us as naked, filthy, ragged, poor, and wretched. Are we then *not* as welcome in his sight as you certainly are in our presence today? On the contrary! That is, if you take Jesus for all eternity as your Savior and Lord. Then you can hear him say: Come naked, come filthy, come ragged, come poor, come wretched, come just as you are.

Welcome!

And may this be a challenge to us to look, as Jesus does, on the heart and not on the outward appearance. Then we can indeed say to one and all—

Welcome!

A General Welcome

(After an appropriate salutation:)

"Do nothing from selfish ambition or conceit, but in humility regard others as better than yourselves" (Phil. 2:3).

As we welcome you here today, we assure you of our high esteem for you, our guests. Thank you for coming; by doing so you have in turn assured us of your high regard for our church, its people, and its pastor.

The program is planned for your participation and enjoyment as we praise God from whom all blessings flow. Your every comfort and need is our command. We want you to be at home with us today. We want you to feel the sweet, sweet Spirit that is in this place and become a part of all that's done.

"Welcome" seems such a small word to express the big feeling we have today, but if you will allow us, we will show you what it means. We will follow the scripture and esteem others, that is you, and you *(point as you speak)* as better than ourselves. Welcome!

Welcome for a
Special Worship Occasion

(After appropriate salutation, including pastors' names, churches in attendance, any special guests, and _____:)

Let us pray:

Eternal God, maker of heaven and earth and creator of us all, we praise you today for the blessings you give. Help us Father to seek you. Help us to seek not just your hand in provision but your face in fellowship. Amen.

As we gather on this special occasion may I remind you of who we serve. This program today is given first of all to honor our Lord and then to minister to our needs as well.

Thank you for coming. You are welcome once, welcome twice, and welcome once again. We assure you of warmth and kindness among God's people as you worship here with us.

Our heart's desire for you today is found in a prayer taken from God's Holy Word, Colossians 1:10: May you "lead lives worthy of the Lord, fully pleasing to him, as you bear fruit in every good work and as you grow in the knowledge of God."

Welcome!

WELCOME FOR CHURCH ANNIVERSARY

Pastors, leaders, friends, Christian brothers and sisters,

We welcome you here today to celebrate the anniversary of this church. We say thank you for coming and we trust that you will feel our warmth and friendliness. It honors us that you would unite with us to mark this special occasion. This church has a long and full history, and we are here today to give credit to Almighty God for having preserved and brought his church to this great day. The church stands as a beacon of light in our community. Indeed, what would the neighborhoods be like without our churches to stand strong against the wiles of the devil? Our churches must take a stand and make a difference. May this great church go forward from this day of celebration to be even better and greater in the years to come.

Again we say welcome to our guests and we intend to meet every possible need you have today for comfort and fellowship on this the anniversary of *(church's name)*.

GENERAL RESPONSE SPEECHES

Response

Christian friends, thank you for your gracious words of welcome. It is wonderful to feel the love that flows in these kind words you have spoken. Words can only express so much, but we have seen you put action to your words. Warm handshakes, friendly smiles, and helpful spirits have reinforced the meaning of your words of welcome. We feel a sense of expectation for what God can do when his family gathers to worship him, and your words of welcome have left no doubt about the family atmosphere here today. We accept your welcome and thank you for your kindness.

Response

Thank you dear Christian brothers and sisters for those kind words of welcome. There is a sweet, sweet Spirit in this place! You have left no doubt that we are loved and accepted in the Beloved here today. It is indeed wonderful when Christians can come together to worship God and find the atmosphere warm with words and deeds of welcome. We thank you for this spirit of welcome, and we praise God for his Holy Spirit of power as we worship him here with you today.

A TRIBUTE

As a loving tribute to _____, let us tell of the life of our friend today. We came here to honor her and what better way to do that than by being reminded of her life.

(Add or subtract details and relationships as appropriate:)

First of all let us speak of her family. They were dear to her heart, and in words and deeds she showed everyone just how dear. There was never a question about her love; it was unselfish, generous to brothers, sisters, nieces, nephews. Truly today her family "rise up and call her blessed" (Prov. 31:28).

Many times we find it easy to love those who are kin, blood relatives, but this one we pay tribute to today loved beyond the circle of her own relatives. Her love included many friends who benefited from her care. One of the qualities she possessed which made her a true friend was her spirit. She never complained, was not negative, and did not condemn others. If a friend shared a mistake or shortcoming, her response was not a shocked put-down but an encouragement to do better next time.

It is important that "all things should be done decently and in order" (1 Cor. 14:40). She conducted her business affairs well, kept her home and property immaculate, and her personal appearance was always pleasant, including her ready smile.

She worked diligently to be a good citizen of the community. Her service as officer of civic organizations is well known. She helped to strengthen, not weaken.

The church certainly played an important role in her life. Her faithful support of its programs and her record of attendance prove her love.

Surely we could continue to name many more accomplishments of our friend. If time and opportunity were given, each of us could tell of specific times and places when our lives were touched by hers.

She lives in our memories and what greater tribute could there be than for us to share her love, joy, giving, positive spirit, and her smile as we continue to serve our families, friends, communities, churches, and our Lord in _____'s honor.

PASTOR'S ANNIVERSARY ADDRESSES

Anniversary

We have come here today to honor our pastor, _____. He is a man of prayer, a man of the Word, a servant of others, and a man of God.

Since he came to us, we have observed him on many occasions. In the pulpit, behind the sacred desk, he delivers God's Word, he preaches the truth. At the bedside of the sick and afflicted in mind and body, he administers comfort, kindness, and healing through God's Holy Spirit. We have found him to be a powerful man of prayer both in his prayer closet and in public prayer. He has stood by many of our families as dear ones pass through the valley of the shadow of death. Faithful is he who endures to the end.

We come to honor him today in our remarks, by our presence, and in whatever small way through gifts and offerings. He is deserving of these tokens of appreciation.

Let us not forget our pastor's beloved helpmate, _____. May we express in a special way our appreciation to and for her. She is faithful to her Lord Jesus, her husband and pastor, and to our church. She graces this and many other occasions with her presence. "A woman who fears the LORD is to be praised" (Prov. 31:30).

And now these closing remarks concerning our pastor:

> O man of God, we can but say
> how you excel in every way!
> Among us now you labor daily,
> Knowing not how he may lead thee.
> Following on in pain and sorrow,
> But looking for that glad tomorrow!

Anniversary

This is a very special occasion in our church. Today we will be celebrating the _____th anniversary of _____ and his wife, _____, as pastor of _____ church.

We come today to pay tribute to them. First of all let me mention six things about _____ which make him so very special.

(Ask young people to hold the letters. They may also be given the statements to make and scripture to read:)

P—He *preaches* God's word with energy and zeal. "Let the elders who rule well be considered worthy of double honor, especially those who labor in preaching and teaching" (1 Tim. 5:17).

A—He *always* points us to God and tells us of his love. "For I am convinced that neither death, nor life, nor angels, nor rulers, nor things present, nor things to come, nor powers, nor height, nor depth, nor anything else in all creation, will be able to separate us from the love of God in Christ Jesus our Lord" (Rom. 8:38-39).

S—His *sermons* make us look at ourselves and ask, "Do we measure up?" "Everyone then who hears these words of mine and acts on them will be like a wise man who built his house on rock" (Matt. 7:24).

T—He *tells* the story of Jesus and his love. "Then Philip began to speak, and starting with this scripture, he proclaimed to him the good news about Jesus" (Acts 8:35).

O—He lives *only* to serve God and minister to *others.* "And he said to him, 'Lord, you know everything; you know that I love you.' Jesus said to him, 'Feed my sheep.' " (John 21:17b).

R—He *responds* to the needs of every member with sweetness and compassion. "By contrast, the fruit of the Spirit is love, joy, peace, patience, kindness, generosity, faithfulness, gentleness, and self-control. There is no law against such things. And those who belong to Christ Jesus have crucified the flesh with its passions and desires. If we live by the Spirit, let us also be guided by the Spirit" (Gal. 5:22-25).

These letters spell "pastor," and he means so much to us! Next I must honor his wife, _____. There are four ways I want to mention in which she is a blessing to our church and its pastor.

- W—Her *wisdom* comes from God above as she seeks him in prayer. "If any of you is lacking in wisdom, ask God, who gives to all generously and ungrudgingly, and it will be given you" (James 1:5).
- I—Her *insight* enables her to know and meet needs for the pastor and the members. "We know that we have passed from death to life because we love one another. Whoever does not love abides in death" (1 John 3:14).
- F—Her *faithfulness* to services, to church organizations, and to her family inspires us all. "Not neglecting to meet together, as is the habit of some, but encouraging one another, and all the more as you see the Day approaching" (Heb. 10:25).
- E—Her *excellence* in whatever she's led to do is a testimony of her obedience. "Many women have done excellently, / but you surpass them all" (Prov. 31:29).

These letters spell "wife," and _____ is the perfect wife for Pastor _____.

May the Lord bless them both with many more years of service and our church with long and strong leadership from our pastor and his wife. I present to you Pastor and Mrs. _____.

First Anniversary

(Slightly altered, this address is appropriate for other anniversaries as well.)

As we come together today to recognize our pastor's first *(or _____)* anniversary, there are many thoughts I would like to express. First of all I'd like to address the fact that she is young, and that is great! It is wonderful to know that God calls and uses young women to serve him.

At the end of your first year as our pastor, I would like to commend you for the way in which you have been faithful to preach God's Word, the Bible, and to love everyone.

There is another special talent you possess, which God has given to you and which you use for his glory. That talent is music. When you play the organ *(or _____)* it is truly as though the harps of heaven are being strummed.

Your love and devotion for and special interest in our choir is dear to me. I appreciate that you have not forgotten where you came from, that you remember the importance of the ministry of music as we worship the Master.

Good people are to be rewarded. I know that we could never repay you for all you are doing, have done, and will continue to do, so I'm asking God to!

USHER DAY ADDRESS

We come today to honor a special group in our church: the Usher Board. Our usher board works hard to make every service an orderly and worshipful experience. Their service to our pastor, us the members, and the Master is a great blessing. They are a blessing to us all year. May we say "God bless you!" to them today. Join me as we say, "God bless you!" *(Congregation responds.)*

Many times we fail to appreciate the behind-the-scenes activity that this group undertakes to make things go smoothly in our services. May we say "Thank you" to them today. Let's say it to them aloud all together: "Thank you!" *(Congregation responds.)*

Sometimes encouragement is needed if workers such as these are to keep being laborers together with God. May we challenge our usher board to "stay faithful" to their calling. Say it with me: "Stay faithful!" *(Congregation responds.)*

On this special occasion we say to our usher board: "God bless you!" "Thank you!" and "Stay faithful!"

INSTALLATION OF OFFICERS

(This program is written as though a member of the organization were doing the installation service. The pronouns can be changed if a nonmember conducts the service.)

President—red ribbon
Vice-president—blue ribbon
Secretary-Treasurer—yellow ribbon
Group leaders or other supporting officers—varying colors, such as orange, green, purple, pink, aqua, lavender, and so on.
Members—differing shades of the colors already used

"Chord of Service"

As we prepare for a new year in our organization, we come at this time to install the officers to serve during the coming year.

We will see illustrated the diversity and the unity of us all as we picture our various duties using the multicolored ribbons to make up the chord of service.

First I will install the president. Duties of the president include presiding at all meetings; appointing and serving on committees as needed; and setting the standard in conduct, participation, and spirit for all other officers and members. Please take the red ribbon to denote your acceptance of this leadership position.

Next we turn to our vice-president. Responsibilities for this office include presiding in the president's absence; assuming committee duties as asked; supporting the president in every way; and holding high values of commitment, service, and loyalty to the organization. Please accept the blue ribbon and by so doing acknowledge your willingness to serve.

Third, our secretary-treasurer will be installed. This office is extremely important. Only as accurate minutes are kept can we know now and in the future what our organization is accomplishing. In keeping trustworthy accounts you will enable us to do many worthwhile projects and be good stewards of our funds. Please take the yellow ribbon and thus indicate your joyful acceptance of this great task.

Each of our group leaders *(or other supporting officers)* fills a strategic position. Your faithfulness to perform whatever duties are needed will make our organization run smoothly and be efficient. Accept these ribbons whose colors are blends of the ones held by our other officers as you promise to fill your supporting roles.

Now to you as members, I ask you also to accept a ribbon, which will be a shade of one of the colors already used. By so doing, pledge yourself to serve when asked, attend regularly, and participate in *your* organizational activities.

As a picture of the beauty and strength of this organization, let us close by making a chord using our multicolored ribbons to remind us of the beauty and strength of this organization when we work together in unity.

MEN'S DAY ADDRESSES

Address

Oh, men of God stand up! We must have Christian, godly, committed men to lead in our churches and in our communities.

We come today to honor and encourage you, the men of our church. How good it is to see you here in God's house today. Somehow, in our culture church attendance and the things of God are not thought of as manly. But how much more macho can you get than to build a boat big enough to hold your own family and pairs of all the creatures on the earth? It took a man of courage to ride out the biggest storm this old world has ever seen as the copilot of that boat and then come out on dry ground ready to reinhabit the whole earth. Noah was a man!

It took a big man to refuse to obey Darius, the mighty Babylonian king, and spend the night surrounded by hungry lions! Men in the early church were tortured and slaughtered, going to their own deaths with manly voices raised in praises to the Lord. Even today there are men who are suffering and dying because they stand immovable in their faith in the living God.

And never was there a *man* such as Jesus! Who "suffered for you, leaving you an example, so that you should follow in his steps. 'He committed no sin, / and no deceit was found in his mouth.' When he was abused, he did not return abuse; when he suffered, he did not threaten; but he entrusted himself to the one who judges justly. He himself bore our sins in his body on the cross, so that, free from sins, we might live for righteousness; by his wounds you have been healed" (1 Pet. 2:21-24). Oh, to be a man like that! Oh, that we would all be men of God like that! We must set the example in this church and in this community of what it really means to be men of God. Oh, men of God stand up!

Address

God is calling for faithful men! In every situation God uses men. For every job God hires men. For every ministry God calls men.

When he chose a people, Abraham was the man he used to be the father of that people. When God needed to preserve a remnant of his people, he hired Noah to build an ark. When the gospel could be shared with the Gentiles, God used the apostle Paul.

Down through history God has used men from all walks of life. He used John Newton, the converted captain of a slave ship, to give us the great hymn "Amazing Grace."

He used William Carey, English shoemaker, to

share Christ in India and begin the modern missionary movement.

And as Martin Luther King, Jr., was preaching the Word in a Baptist church in Atlanta, God inspired him to lead the great civil rights movement all across America.

Who is here today that God wants to use? In our church and in our community God is calling faithful men. Hear him when he says, "Who will go for me and who can I send?" And by the grace of God, assured of our prayers and support, answer him, "Here am I, Lord, send me!"

WOMEN'S DAY ADDRESS

We come today to honor the women of our church. We are honoring women who are faithful both to our Lord and to *(name of the church)*.

Let me mention some qualities that exemplify the faithfulness of these women. At many services the women of our church far outnumber all others in attendance. Next they give both of time and money, many from limited incomes. May God bless them richly! And last they are leaders. Without the women who lead we could never have the activities which enrich the life of our church. Just for instance, what would our choir be without faithful women?

All that I have said is true and important, but let me close by telling you the most important reason we are honoring these women today. They are God's servants! He called them to be women who serve him! That service comes from the love of God!

The scripture says, "Whoever serves me must follow me, and where I am, there will my servant be also. Whoever serves me, the Father will honor" (John 12:26).

FAMILY DAY ADDRESS

God ordained the family as an institution when he created Adam and gave him a helpmate, Eve. In our culture today, the traditional family—Dad, Mom, and the kids—is the exception rather than the rule. We must include, support, and honor those single-parent families as well. Their needs are great and their courage challenges us.

We come today to pay tribute to *the family.* The needs of the family are represented by three L's—Laws, Love, and Levels. *(You may wish to print these three words on poster board, and then ask a young person to display them one at a time or place them one by one on an easel. This would be a helpful visual aid to your presentation.)*

First of all for a family to function well it must have *laws.* The Bible says in the Ten Commandments, "Honor your father and your mother." And again in the New Testament we find, "Children, obey your parents in the Lord, for this is right" (Eph. 6:1). The laws or standards set up should include attending school and making acceptable grades as well as having good conduct, being faithful to church activities, and doing chores to help the home run smoothly. God's laws or standards apply not only to the children, but also to the parents, who are to submit to God and to each other (Eph. 5:21), being faithful to provide a secure home and lead in spiritual life.

Then there is *love:* love for one another and love

for God. This is the kind of love that sacrifices what one family member may want for the greater good of the whole family.

Love from your family is undeserved.
They love you because you are one of their own.
How precious to have a place reserved
Where you are loved just for you and not for what you have done.

A family's love must also be tough love! Love that demands your best and helps you achieve it. Love that will not accept the unacceptable, yet a love that never stops loving.

Finally a family provides the foundation for all *levels* of achievement. Just as the Bible says of itself, "All Scripture is inspired by God and is useful for teaching, for reproof, for correction, and for training in righteousness, so that everyone who belongs to God may be proficient, equipped for every good work," the family is provided so that we may be complete and equipped for reaching our full potential. To produce good citizens, who are working, functioning, caring adults, should be the goal of all parents concerning their children. A godly family provides the launching pad that will rocket our young people to high levels of success.

In closing may I commend those families who have the three L's—laws, love, and levels. And may I challenge us all to be a part of enforcing and reinforcing these values in our own families and those of others.

Skits Useful for Demonstrating the Three L's

Laws

Mom: Johnny, are you dressed yet? We are going to be late to church.

Johnny: *(wearing sloppy, radical clothes)* Naw, Mom. I don't like what you said I had to wear and besides I don't think I'll go to church today.

Mom: No, dressed like that you won't! Let me ask you something—Is it Sunday?

Johnny: Sure it's Sunday.

Mom: Well then let's get something straight. If it's Sunday we are going to church. You don't have to wonder, you don't have to ask. If it's Sunday we *are going* to church! *(Johnny begins to look shocked at Mom's excitement.)* And another thing—if it's Monday you are going to school! You don't have to wonder, you don't have to ask! Any day Monday through Friday if school is in session *you are* going! *(By this time he has dropped his head and is shuffling his feet.)* And since I'm a good Baptist *(or _____)* and we have three points in our sermon—don't you ever ask for a motorcycle, because you're not going to get one! *(Moving up closer to Johnny, gesturing with hand, perhaps pointing finger in his face.)*

Johnny: *(Looks amazed. Begins to change clothes to get ready to go to church.)* Yes Ma'am!

Unconditional Love

Father: Well, Son are you O.K.?

Son: Yeah, Dad, I'm fine. Just stupid is all!

Father: Now I don't want to hear any talk like that. Anyone can get turned around and go the wrong way.

Son: But in a gym, during a game, with the championship on the line, and score the winning basket for the other team? I really goofed!

Father: Yes, you made a mistake.

Son: I don't ever want to leave this house, this room again. You and Mom can just set my food outside the door and I'll get it later so you won't have to look at me.

Father: What about school?

Son: Oh, I'm not going back there anymore! Did you hear what they were calling me? Wrong-way Williamson! I'll never live that down.

Father: I know it won't be easy but what I want you to do is stand up straight, smile, hold your head up, and not let this get you down. I love you! I loved you before you made this mistake and I still love you. No matter what

I'll always love you! You know what? *(Son shakes his head, no.)* Jesus loves you too!

Son: *(smiling)* O.K. Dad, I guess with you on my side, and Jesus too, I can at least try again.

Father: That's my boy!

Levels

(Young woman dressed neatly in a business suit; the image of success. Young man in a uniform. Sharp. Both have Bibles in hand. Older person sitting in a chair.)

Older Person: I certainly am glad you two young people came to church today. I would have been so sorry if you had not let me see you! My you are looking good.

Young Woman: Thank you. It's a joy to see you too.

Young Man: It certainly is, Ma'am.

Older Person: I can see the Lord is blessing you. Tell me about it.

Young Man: Well, with the encouragement of my family and other Christian adults like you I have been able to achieve a lot. I am serving my country, receiving training, and being able to grow in my life as a Christian. I attend a wonderful church where I'm stationed.

	The devil doesn't like anything about my life, and I give God the glory because he used people just like you to equip me to reach this level of life and go on even higher!
Older Person:	Praise the Lord!
Young Woman:	I too have you, the church, my family, but most of all our God to thank for anything I may have accomplished. I have a good job with responsibility and influence on the lives of others. But my achievements belong to others!
Older Person:	God bless you! You know, Satan trembles when he sees two young people as fine as you are!

SACRIFICIAL LOVE

(Tableau of a woman sewing. Narrator speaks.)

She sits in the dim light, her head bent over her work long after everyone else has gone to sleep. Not just occasionally, but almost every night she sits and works like this until the wee hours of the morning. Her head hurts, her eyes burn, her back aches *(appropriate gestures)*. Still she works on. This is not her only job. She works all day outside her home and then comes home to care for her family's needs before she spends a long evening doing this tedious labor. Why? *(Woman looks up and smiles with a faraway expression.)* Her reasons are good ones. A better education and an easier life for her children head the list. She is sacrificing her ease, comfort, time, even her health to benefit other members of her family. "I give you a new commandment, that you love one another. Just as I have loved you, you also should love one another" (John 13:34). This is sacrificial love!

CHOIR DAY ADDRESS

As we come to observe the annual Choir Day in our church, I have been blessed with the opportunity to share some of my thoughts about our choir.

The word "choir" brings pictures to our minds. We visualize many individual members, clothed in beautiful robes, raising different voices to sing the hymns of our faith, accompanied by various instruments. We picture the choir, but have you ever thought of the significance of each item in that picture? Today I would like to talk about each one: the robes, the voices, the hymns, the instruments.

Why does our choir wear robes? Obviously they are attractive, bright, and colorful. But the significance goes much deeper. The choir is a unit, a team, and by dressing alike, its members appear as one. "We are one in the Spirit, we are one in the Lord." Instead of each member being responsible for dressing appropriately for worship services and other occasions, each one is clothed in a robe. Isaiah 61:10 says, "He has covered me with the robe of righteousness," and in Revelation 7:9 we are told that we will stand "before the throne and before the Lamb, robed in white." It seems that the unity displayed by the robes our choir wears here today speaks of the great union of all the saints for eternity!

Doesn't it thrill your heart when our choir members raise their voices in praise to our Lord? Voices are God-given blessings, quite significant because they allow us to sing of our Redeemer! "There are glad songs of victory in the tents of the righteous" (Ps. 118:15).

The hymns our choir sings are significant because of what the Bible says about them. Colossians 3:16 tells us, "Let the Word of Christ dwell in you richly; teach and admonish one another in all wisdom; and with gratitude in your hearts sing psalms, hymns, and spiritual songs to God." What our choir sings is indeed important. They sing hymns of Jesus and his love! Singing hymns is also emphasized in scripture when we are told, "When they had sung the hymn, they went out to the Mount of Olives" (Matt. 26:30). Jesus and his disciples after the Last Supper sang a hymn.

Instruments add beautiful accompaniment to our choir. Do they have special significance? Oh, yes! The blending of music from piano, organ, drum, guitar, cymbals, and tambourines with human voices fills the place with melody. Psalm 150:4 tells us to "praise him with strings and pipe," and Isaiah 38:20 says, "We will sing to stringed instruments / all the days of our lives, / at the house of the LORD."

The picture is complete and now you know that there is a good reason, a Bible-based reason, why our wonderful choir is clothed in beautiful robes, why its members raise their voices to sing hymns about Jesus accompanied by instruments of praise.

THE FIVE F'S OF FRIENDSHIP

Faithful   Fruitful   Funloving   Fearless   Faultless

We come here today to celebrate Friend's Day. We need to look at two aspects of friendship in order for our program to address each and every one of us. We must not only give honor, thanks, and rewards to someone who has befriended us, but also be a friend to someone else. Pass it on!

In seeking to turn our thoughts to what true friendship is may I suggest five words which describe friendship? So that our memories might be aided, each of these words begins with F.

A friend must be *faithful;* one who is loyal and true, one who can be depended on in every situation. Many good friendships last for years, span distances, and survive changes. Faithful is the friend who stands by through joy and sorrow never wavering, but always being there when you need a friend.

Friendship is *fruitful.* There are rewards to both the friend and the one befriended. When you perform deeds of friendship you sow seeds of kindness, which reap a rich reward. The Bible says in Galatians 6:7, "You reap whatever you sow." We often think of that in a negative way, but the principle certainly holds true for *good* seed and *good* fruit.

How delicious the taste of a ripe, juicy peach or a crisp, red apple! Fruitful acts of friendship are even more pleasant. "By contrast, the fruit of the Spirit is love, joy, peace, patience, kindness, generosity, faithfulness, gentleness, and self-control" (Gal. 5:22-23). Today we honor and encourage joyfully sowing the seeds of friendship and enjoying the fruit they produce!

Funloving is the next word we are using to describe friendship. Laughter is important! Proverbs 17:22 says, "A cheerful heart is a good medicine." Being able to laugh at ourselves, and make other people laugh, is a gift. Friendships are made rich and rewarding by sharing the gift of laughter.

"Fear not, for I am with you" is spoken of our Lord and his constant presence with us. Oh how great a comfort to be joined by a friend when we are in a fearful situation. True friendship makes us *fearless!*

No one likes to be criticized. Friends are encouragers, not discouragers. *Faultless* is the word that describes a friend who always sees the positive but never accents the negative. Be a fault-overlooker instead of a fault-finder and you will be a friend and have many friends.

We have looked at the five F's of friendship: Faithful, Fruitful, Funloving, Fearless, and Faultless. May each of us go away from this place with a new commitment to true friendship. "A *friend* loveth at all times!"

THE WALK OF FAITH

(For this presentation, choose someone to respond to the narrator's questions.)

Take a walk with me for a while down a little road. As I walk, wondering what I can do for Jesus, I see a man preaching. He has the Bible open to the book of the Law. Some stop to listen and pass on by, but a few stay to hear him out. He knows what he's talking about and speaks boldly. If he were a lawyer I think he would be successful, or he might be a prominent doctor in the city, or make a million dollars as a businessman.

Narrator: Sir, what is your name?

Isaiah: My name is Isaiah.

Narrator: Well, Isaiah, what are you doing?

Isaiah: I'm preaching to the people!

Narrator: And you're doing a good job, but I'm afraid you aren't being appreciated!

Isaiah: But sir, I'm not doing it to be appreciated.

Narrator: Why not? That's not normal.

Isaiah: Well, back when King Uzziah died I saw the Lord, holy and lifted up, and I said "Woe is me," but an angel took a live coal from the altar and put it on my mouth, and I could not help preaching! I couldn't be a lawyer, doctor, businessman, or anything else because the fire of God is on my lips. I have seen him who is invisible!

41

I shake my head in puzzlement and walk on a little farther to where another little fellow is preaching. All of a sudden the crowd begins to throw rocks at him and he falls to the ground. I am able to cradle his bloody head and speak to him a moment before he dies.

Narrator: What is your name?

Stephen: My name is Stephen *(with a smile).*

Narrator: Oh, sir you ought not to be smiling, you are dying! What are you, Stephen?

Stephen: I am a deacon!

Narrator: A deacon? But I saw you preaching.

Stephen: I'm a preaching deacon.

Narrator: It seems to me you ought to be in a committee meeting somewhere telling the pastor how to run the church.

Stephen: No, God didn't call me because I was a good businessman. He didn't call me because I was smart. He called me because I was full of the Holy Ghost.

Narrator: The blows to your head have clouded your thoughts.

Stephen: I see the glory of God! Jesus is standing at the right hand of God!

Narrator: Oh, Stephen, every good deacon knows that Jesus is *sitting* at the right hand of God.

Stephen: Yes, but he's standing up to welcome me! I'm so glad I did what I did, because I've seen him who is invisible!

As I continue my walk I come upon three young men in a fiery furnace. They give me their names as Shadrach, Meshach, and Abednego. *(Each one bows.)*

Narrator: Weren't you fellows chosen to be leaders during the captivity of the Jews in Babylon? I thought you were headed for the top. What happened?

Shadrach: We refused to pray and bow down to the statue of the king. Here he comes now.

King: Why aren't you three burned to a crisp? Wait—there are four men in the furnace!

Shadrach: Sir, the extra one is he who is invisible!

I walk farther and see an old, gray-haired man who hasn't had a haircut in years. His beard is on his chest and blends with the hairs of his head. He has the sweetest expression on his face I've ever seen!

Narrator: Sir, what is the population of this island?

John: One.

Narrator: Oh, you must have misunderstood the question. How many people live here?

John: One.

Narrator: Then you must be the one.

John: Yes.

Narrator: Well, you have my love, appreciation, and sympathy. I know you must get very lonely.

John: Lonely? Oh, no, I've seen seraphim and cherubim, the great wedding feast for the marriage of the Lamb. I've seen saints coming in the clouds on white horses and the golden streets of the new Jerusalem!

Narrator: Sometimes when you get up in years you have hallucinations like that.

John: Don't worry about me. All these years I've been out here I have been seeing him who is invisible.

Now I see a little fellow leading a band of Israelites.

Narrator: Moses, aren't you the young man who was raised in Pharaoh's palace?

Moses: Yes, sir, I am.

Narrator: This hiking in the desert must be your hobby since you're the head of a great kingdom.

Moses: I am not welcome in the palace.

Narrator: What happened?

Moses: I killed an Egyptian and had to flee for my life. One day I was keeping some sheep in the wilderness when I saw a burning bush; it burned but never burned down. Then in that bush as I approached it, I saw him who is invisible.

Narrator: But, Moses, don't you realize you could be the Pharaoh in Egypt?

Moses: No, I could not be disobedient to the heavenly vision, because I've seen him who is invisible.

Isaiah gave up prominence and wealth to preach an unpopular message, Stephen refused to play church politics and lost his life, the Hebrew men chanced death rather than disobey, John became an outcast, and Moses relinquished a throne all because of faith in him who is invisible. *(Each one steps forward as name is called.)*

Read Hebrews 11:24-27.

A GODLY WOMAN

Sarah was a faithful wife.
Rebekah followed obediently.
Rahab protected her family.
Ruth spells trust even today.
Could there be a better-balanced woman than the
    Proverbs 31 woman?
Mary was chosen to be the mother of Christ!
Another Mary was the first to see him back alive!
Priscilla was a giant in the early church.
Lois and Eunice trained a young preacher.

What about you? Oh, woman of today?
What are you doing to glorify God?
Use these Bible women as examples to be—
The kind of a woman called godly.

NINE KEYS TO GOD'S RESOURCES

1. God gives life that is *everlasting*.
2. God gives *unity* to draw us together in one body.
3. God gives *forgiveness* for all our sins.
4. Because of God's gift of Christ we bear the name *Christian*.
5. God gives *wisdom* beyond understanding.
6. In place of *discouragement* God gives hope for every tomorrow.
7. God gives *peace* in the midst of the storm.
8. God gives *love* that is perfect because God is love.
9. And God gives *courage* to face whatever may come.

STEWARDSHIP

God has a plan for giving to his church. That plan for giving is laid out for us in the Bible. Malachi 3:10 says, "Bring the full tithe into the storehouse." The word "tithe" means one tenth, and the word "storehouse" as used in our culture today means the local church.

Therefore we are given a guideline to use to determine how God wants us to give. Just to make this as simple as possible, suppose your paycheck this week from that good job God has given you reads $350! Praise the Lord! Isn't that a wonderful blessing? Just take $35 of that $350 and give it to the church; in doing so, according to Malachi 3:10, you will be tithing! Sometimes you may be able to give more by making an offering for some special need. Then you are following the scripture that says "God loves a cheerful giver" (2 Cor. 9:7).

Is there more to stewardship than just money? I believe the answer is yes! God has given each of us gifts. The time and effort we expend ministering with these gifts is part of being a good steward. What about the children you have been given? Give them back to God in dedication and in teaching them to trust and obey him.

As you can see, stewardship involves every part of our lives. It begins with our money, which many times becomes a symbol of our relationship to God. Let us be good stewards and obey God's Word, which says, "Give . . . to God the things that are God's" (Matt. 22:21; Mark 12:17; Luke 20:25).

HOW TO KNOW GOD

"Jesus is the one who delivers us daily from our sins and shame." He takes our lives and makes of them something beautiful. We are nothing, but in him we have worth and value.

His love constrains us and makes us willing to love others, even the unlovely. How can we thank him for the free gift of eternal life he gives? We can commit our lives to him, let him be Lord, and practice his presence every moment.

There is so much busyness and clutter in our world today. We must work to carve out a haven where he reigns and rules. Our homes, our churches, and whatever portion of schools and businesses we have influence in should be these havens of rest. The world is so noisy and cruel. People need quiet, peaceful, kind places to spend some time.

Is your home filled with sounds every moment? Are there televisions, stereos, radios, phones ringing, voices raised, constant bickering? Turn off the source of all this confusion and tune in to the quietness that fills God's world. He says, "Be still, and know that I am God" (Ps. 46:10). It is no wonder more people don't really know God today if being still and quiet is the way to do so.

TWO BLESSINGS

You have heard people speak of "the second blessing." The Bible also tells of two blessings, but not perhaps the ones you think.

It is obvious that God blesses. Even those who do not claim to be God-fearers are aware of his blessings all around them. The scripture says that God "sends rain on the righteous and on the unrighteous" (Matt. 5:45).

You are blessed by God as a believer—in many more ways than with just the general blessings of the creation. His love abounds toward you, and you experience abundant life here and now and eternal life and blessing in heaven forever.

Let us now deal with the second blessing as the scripture does. Acts 1:8 says, "But you will receive power when the Holy Spirit has come upon you." You are blessed! It continues, "And you will be my witnesses in Jerusalem, in all Judea and Samaria, and to the ends of the earth." You are blessed in order to be a blessing!

You are given blessings not so you can hoard them, or turn them over in your hands and admire them; not even merely to preserve them and keep them on display. You are blessed to bless others.

The Acts account is only one time God sets forth this principle. Again in Luke 24:48, he says, "You are witnesses," and in 24:50, "Lifting up his hands, he blessed them." And in Matthew 28:19-20, he says, "Go therefore and make disciples of all nations, baptizing them in the name of the Father and of the Son and of the Holy Spirit, and teaching them to obey everything that I have commanded you. And remember, I am with you always, to the end of the age."

Each time the principle is present the double blessing is evident. Why are you blessed? So that you can be a blessing. You have so much, but so many have nothing. You are blessed, yes, you have only to look and see all around you how God has blessed you. But do you not think God will require of you an account of your handling of the blessing?

A PLAN OF SALVATION

In the beginning God created the heavens and the earth.[a] God also made Adam and Eve,[b] and desired to have fellowship with them. This was true for a while.[c] Then Adam and Eve listened to Satan's lies and were driven from the presence of God.[d]

There existed a huge gulf between God and man.[e,f] The only way there could be communion and fellowship between them was to bridge the gap.[g] This was done when God sent Jesus.[h] He came to earth as the God-man, God in human flesh,[i] so that when he lived a sinless life[j] and died on the cross, was buried and arose from the grave, he built that bridge.[k]

As I accept, believe, and appropriate his life, death, and resurrection,[l] I become a new creature,[m] able once more to fellowship with God. My obedience causes me to grow[n] as I come to know him more fully[o] and prepare to spend eternity with him in heaven.[p]

a. Genesis 1:1
b. Genesis 1:27
c. Genesis 3:8
d. Genesis 3:23
e. Isaiah 59:2
f. Luke 16:26
g. Hebrews 7:19
h. John 3:17
i. John 10:38
j. 1 Peter 2:22
k. 1 Corinthians 15:3-4
l. Romans 10:9, 10, 13
m. 2 Corinthians 5:17
n. John 14:23
o. Philippians 3:10
p. 1 Thessalonians 4:17

A FRIEND LOVETH AT ALL TIMES

I am weak and heavy burdened.
I am sick and wracked with pain.
I am lonely and need a listener.
Dear Lord, hear me and send a friend.

I am blessed and must tell someone.
I have joy to sing about.
Oh, the peace that floods my being!
Dear Lord, hear me and send my friend.

I have love that needs an outlet.
I have gifts that I must give.
I am full to overflowing!
Dear Lord, hear me and make me a friend.

GOD WILL PROVIDE

Whatever your needs are, God will provide.
He'll guard you, sustain you, and he'll be your guide.
Our needs are so many,
But he spares not any.
Trust and obey now,
And no want will he allow.

When you are sick, and when you are lonely,
Count on God, and him only.
There are those who would do you harm,
But with God's protection, sound no alarm.
In the midst of your need,
You stand in liberty, freed!

Yes, in every situation,
God is in charge of liberation!
Whether needs are great or small
God's the sustainer of us all.
In life and in death, he will provide
When we choose with him to abide.

REDEEMING LOVE

"Redeeming love has been my theme and will be 'til I die."

What does it mean to redeem? It can mean to buy back, as in the case of slaves having been redeemed from a cruel master and given their freedom. Redeeming the time can mean turning off the television and reading God's Word or a good book. It can be spending quality time talking to your husband, wife, or child or playing a game together. To redeem a piece of property, you pay off the mortgage.

How about a soul though? How can a soul be redeemed? "All we like sheep have gone astray; / we have all turned to our own way, / and the LORD has laid on him [Jesus] / the iniquity of us all" (Isa. 53:6). We were in bondage to Satan, and God allowed the blood of his precious Son to buy us back and set us free! "God did not send the Son into the world to condemn the world, but in order that the world might be saved through him" (John 3:17).

We have talked about the word "redeem"; now let's put the phrase together—redeeming love. Many times we can understand a concept better by seeing it fleshed out in the life of a person. Look with me at an example of redeeming love.

William Carey, missionary to India, because of God's redeeming love to him gave a lifetime of service to God. He spent ten years translating the Bible into languages the Indians could understand; it was thirteen years before he saw the first Indian convert. During a cholera epidemic when he and his wife were deathly ill, their small child died and no one would suffer defilement in order to bury the little fellow. Mrs. Carey went insane and had to be restrained to keep her from hurting herself. Still he worked on.

In India at that time, whenever a Hindu man died, his widow, no matter how young (many were only twelve or thirteen) was burned along with him on the burial fire. In celebration of a certain goddess's feast, many girl infants were sacrificed. William Carey, because of God's redeeming love, fought these practices and finally persuaded the government to outlaw them!

Redeeming love like William Carey's as lived out in India should inspire us to try God's redeeming love right where we live. I challenge you to heed the words of the hymn and make redeeming love your theme until you die.

BORROWED

They borrowed a bed to lay His head,
When Christ the Lord came down,
They borrowed an ass in the mountain pass
For Him to ride to town.
  But the crown that He wore
  And the cross that He bore
    Were His own.

He borrowed the bread when the crowd He fed
On the grassy mountain side;
He borrowed the dish of broken fish
With which He satisfied.
  But the crown that He wore
  And the cross that He bore
    Were His own.

He borrowed the ship in which to sit
To teach the multitude,
He borrowed the nest in which to rest,
He had never a home as rude,
  But the crown that He wore
  And the cross that He bore
    Were His own.

He borrowed a room on the way to the tomb,
The passover lamb to eat.
They borrowed a cave, for Him a grave,

They borrowed a winding sheet.
   But the crown that He wore
   And the cross that He bore
     Were His own.

The thorns on His head were worn in my stead,
For me the Saviour died;
For guilt of my sin the nails drove in
When Him they crucified.
   Though the crown that He wore
   And the cross that He bore
     Were His own,
They rightly were mine—instead.

—*Anonymous*

GOD'S WILL FOR US

Just to be tender, just to be true;
Just to be glad the whole day through;
Just to be merciful, just to be mild;
Just to be trustful as a child;
Just to be gentle and kind and sweet;
Just to be helpful with willing feet;
Just to be cheery when things go wrong;
Just to drive sadness away with a song,
Whether the hour is dark or bright;
Just to be loyal to God and right;
Just to believe that God knows best;
Just in His promise ever to rest;
Just to let love be our daily key;
This is God's will, for you and me.

—Anonymous